D1715063

Ballads of the Old West

A Collection of Story Poems

Jean Johenning

Featuring 16 full-page illustrations
by Western artist W. R. "Dick" Doherty

VANTAGE PRESS
New York

Published by Vantage Press, Inc.
516 West 34th Street, New York, New York 10001

Manufactured in the United States of America
ISBN: 0-533-10320-7

Library of Congress Catalog Card No.: 92-90789

0 9 8 7 6 5 4 3 2 1

To Mom and Ralph

Contents

Acknowledgements

I wish to thank most sincerely W. R. "Dick" Doherty of Delta, Colorado, for his splendid artwork, which has been such a wonderful asset in helping my ballads spring to life off the printed page.

I also express my gratitude to Bea Roeder and the people at Arvada Center For The Arts and Humantities near Denver for the opportunities they have offered me to present my ballads aloud at their annual event, the Colorado Cowboy Poetry Gathering.

Introduction

Hello, my name is Jean Johenning and I write ballads, story poems about the Old West. I want to continue in the tradition of that great ballad-maker Robert Service. He wrote about the snow-covered wastelands of the Yukon. My own specialty is the American West, although several of my ballads are also set in Robert Service's land of the north.

Stagecoaches, gunfighters, sheriffs, gold and silver mines, lovely ladies, cattle drives, these are the stuff of which legends—and ballads—are made. Come with me now into my world of story-telling in meter and rhyme as we relive some fictional tales of the Western frontier.

But first let me tell you a few points about how I write a ballad. The most important matter of all—and the hardest part—is getting a good story. I have written between twenty and thirty ballads, most of which are about the Old West. But I would have a far greater total if I could come up more easily with interesting and exciting tales. New stories are indeed hard to come by.

Even after creating a tentative story, the ballad-maker still must stress having a memorable climax, which fulfills the promise of the story and adds excellence to the ballad as a whole. Actually, there is another approach that I sometimes use: writing the final couplet *first*, which assures me of an effective ending, and then writing a story that leads up to this final couplet. (Any method that can produce results!)

After developing the outline of a good story, the author then has to fill in the details and reach a climax as the poet sets down the story in meter and rhyme—the traditional format of most ballads, especially those of Robert Service. One of the main reasons for this is that ballads are meant to be heard aloud. The meter and rhyme create a music and a rhythm as the adventure is related orally.

Titles are another important item, for they should capture the interest of the readers/listeners right from the start. When you see such titles as "The Nugget of Gold," "Stagecoach to Cheyenne," or "The Double Hanging," I hope you will be thinking to yourself, "Hey, I wonder what that story is all about."

So may every reader enjoy the story poems in this book. But, partners, we'll have a lot more fun if we can get together some day and I can present my ballads for you aloud. That's when characters like Old Whiskers McCoy, Vermont Valentine, Sheriff Tom Cleet, and Virginia Nash will really come to life. So let's look forward to the time when we can get together for an oral presentation of some of my ballads. In this way we are actually continuing the oral tradition of poetic literature, which goes back even before the days of the ancient Greek Homer.

But until we do meet, good luck with your reading of these ballads. And if you come up with some thought-provoking story about the Old West, let me know about it. Perhaps together we can create another exciting ballad about the wonderful personalities and characters of the American Western frontier.

Onward to Kansas City and points West!

Jean Johenning
105 Stewart Ave.
Garden City, NY 11530
(516) 354-5674

Ballads of the Old West

Cast of Characters and Places of Interest

B

Beautiful Belle—Dealer in high-stakes poker game between Whiskers McCoy and Vermont Valentine ("The Nugget of Gold").

Roscoe Beck—Gets into argument with Tom Price at poker game ("Cold Blue Eyes of Steel").

Big Moose Mine—Site of murder and payroll robbery ("Legend of the Northwest").

Frankie Bly—Stands up for a "gal with blue eyes" when she is mistreated by Big Tom McLarn ("The Memory of Blue").

Swifty Bryant—Gambling hall owner who gambles at roulette against both Dan McGowan and Bobby Macon ("A Game of Roulette").

Bryant's Gambling Hall—Scene of famous roulette game. Owned by Swifty Bryant ("A Game of Roulette").

Joe Bucket—Brings message from the Norton Brothers to Sheriff Tom Cleet ("Facing the Test").

C

Pepper Carney—Prospector who takes his nephew Bucky Coe to the Yukon to search for gold ("To Look Death in the Eye").

Clark—Shot down by Bill Park at Big Moose Mine ("Legend of the Northwest").

Sheriff Tom Cleet—Confronts the Norton Brothers in shootout at the Red Hat Saloon ("Facing the Test").

Bucky Coe—Faces thrills and adventure with his uncle in the Yukon. But when he returns to San Francisco . . . ("To Look Death in the Eye").

D

Dallas Blue—Bobby Kean's sweetheart, famous for her eyes of blue ("A Gal Named Dallas Blue").

Dangerous Blue—The wildest bucking bronco in all the West ("Dangerous Blue").

Charles Dillon—Unlucky gambler heading for Cheyenne ("Stagecoach to Cheyenne").

Sheriff Douglas—Lawman who investigates the murder of Tim McPhee ("The Double Hanging").

Lilly Drew—Marries Sheriff Rex McNeil ("Cold Blue Eyes of Steel").

F

Clyde and Jason Fletcher—Brothers who confront Lou LeMaire about June LaDue ("No Day for a Hanging").

Bill Ford—Horse thief pursued by Sheriff Rex McNeil ("Cold Blue Eyes of Steel").

G

"Gal with Blue Eyes"—Source of argument between Frankie Bly and Big Tom McLarn ("The Memory of Blue").

H

Robby Halpen—Suspect in murder of gambler Tim McPhee ("The Double Hanging").

Buster Hancock—The man Charles McKenna is accused of murdering ("The Ace of Spades").

Peter Hatchet—Assists Sheriff Douglas in the investigation of the Tim McPhee murder ("The Double Hanging").

Kathy Hughes—Bart Ringo's dark-haired girlfriend whom he later marries ("The Ace of Spades").

J

Charlie Johnson—Promises wild party if he succeeds in riding Dangerous Blue at the Durango rodeo ("Dangerous Blue").

K

Mary Kane—Robby Halpen's blue-eyed girlfriend ("The Double Hanging").

Bobby Kean—The cowboy loved by Dallas Blue ("A Gal Named Dallas Blue").

L

June LaDue—Marries Lou LeMaire ("No Day for a Hanging").

Lou LeMaire—Farmer who twice helps Jake O'Dunn in time of need ("No Day for a Hanging").

M

Sergeant Mackenzie—Member of Northwest Mounted Police (Mountie) who pursues Bill Park in a blizzard ("Legend of the Northwest").

Bobby Macon—Cowboy who puts up his ranch in roulette game against Swifty Bryant ("A Game of Roulette").

Mason Brothers—Once held up the stagecoach to Cheyenne ("Stagecoach to Cheyenne").

Tom McCall—Robs bank and is pursued by the Pike Brothers ("To Flip a Coin").

Kate McCoy—Marries Billy Pike ("To Flip a Coin").

Old Whiskers McCoy—Discovers a nugget of gold and tries to win it in a poker game with Vermont Valentine ("The Nugget of Gold").

Little Luke McDonough—Has heavy mortgage on ranch outside Durango. Attempts to ride Dangerous Blue at rodeo ("Dangerous Blue").

Dan McGowan—Debt-ridden rancher who tries to improve his fortunes by winning at roulette ("A Game of Roulette").

Marilla McGowan—Wife of Dan McGowan ("A Game of Roulette").

Sue McGowan—Brown-eyed daughter of Dan McGowan who is sought after by both Swifty Bryant and Bobby Macon ("A Game of Roulette").

Slim Jim McGunn—Shot down by Norton Brothers at Red Hat Saloon ("Facing the Test").

Charles McKenna—Stagecoach driver accused of murder. Famous for ace of spades stuck in the band of his hat ("The Ace of Spades").

Big Tom McLarn—Fights Frankie Bly at the Walk In Saloon ("The Memory of Blue").

Rex McNeil—Sheriff at Dallas, Texas, famous for his cold blue eyes of steel ("Cold Blue Eyes of Steel").

Tim McPhee—Gambler shot down at card game—but who is guilty? ("The Double Hanging").

Roscoe Morgan—Dies attempting train robbery ("The Last Bullet").

Murphy's Grand Saloon—Site of controversial poker game ("Cold Blue Eyes of Steel").

N

Tom Nash—Tavern owner and father of Virginia Nash ("Love Me 'Til I Die").

Virginia Nash—Famous for her singing of the song "Love Me 'Til I Die" at her father's tavern. Disappears mysteriously ("Love Me 'Til I Die").

Big Norton Brothers—Challenge Sheriff Tom Cleet to six-shooter showdown at the Red Hat Saloon ("Facing the Test").

O

Peg O'Brien—Hopes to marry Buck Ray in Cheyenne ("Stagecoach to Cheyenne").

Jake O'Dunn—Close friend of Lou LeMaire. Arrested as a horse thief ("No Day for a Hanging").

P

Bill Park—Shoots down Clark at the Big Moose Mine and flees with the payroll ("Legend of the Northwest").

Billy Parker—Texan who tries to ride Dangerous Blue at the Durango rodeo ("Dangerous Blue").

Spider Parker—Train robber ("The Last Bullet").

Billy Pike—Deputy to his brother Sheriff Stephen Pike in Santa Fe, New Mexico ("To Flip a Coin").

Stephen Pike—Brother of Billy Pike and sheriff of Santa Fe. Noted for making important decisions by flipping a coin ("To Flip a Coin").

Willie Piper—Rider on stagecoach to Cheyenne. Had no luck in seeking gold near Denver ("Stagecoach to Cheyenne").

Tom Price—Wins final poker pot at Murphy's Grand Saloon ("Cold Blue Eyes of Steel").

R

Philip Randall—Real estate speculator heading for Cheyenne ("Stagecoach to Cheyenne").

Buck Ray—Followed to Cheyenne by Peg O'Brien ("Stagecoach to Cheyenne").

Red Hat Saloon—Location of shootout between the Norton Brothers and Sheriff Tom Cleet ("Facing the Test").

Bart Ringo—Charles McKenna's best friend who rides shotgun with him on the Arizona stage ("The Ace of Spades").

S

Thomas Shea—Held up while transporting a shipment of gold by train to Denver ("The Last Bullet").

Sled—Rides shotgun next to the driver Thomas Wilson on the stagecoach to Cheyenne ("Stagecoach to Cheyenne").

Rodney Sloth—Robby Halpen's best friend. Also a suspect in the murder of Tim McPhee ("The Double Hanging").

Robert Smith—Seeks election to political office at Cheyenne ("Stagecoach to Cheyenne").

Stallion Ranch—Ranch near Dallas where Rex McNeil worked before becoming sheriff ("Cold Blue Eyes of Steel").

The Stranger—Attempts to rob Bucky Coe and Pepper Carney of their gold ("To Look Death in the Eye").

T

Judge Mathias Turner—Timekeeper when rodeo riders try to stay on Dangerous Blue for twelve seconds ("Dangerous Blue").

V

Vermont Valentine—Gold prospector, along with his best friend, Whiskers McCoy. Plays poker game to win the nugget of gold ("The Nugget of Gold").

W

Walk In Saloon—Site of fight between Frankie Bly and Big Tom McLarn ("The Memory of Blue").

Wandering Stranger Saloon—Site of poker game between Whiskers McCoy and Vermont Valentine ("The Nugget of Gold").

Webster Brothers—Train robbers ("The Last Bullet").

Thomas Wilson—Driver of stagecoach to Cheyenne ("Stagecoach to Cheyenne").

1. The Nugget of Gold

Old Whiskers McCoy and Vermont Valentine
Dreamed elegant dreams of the splendid gold mine
That they'd find some day if their luck would prevail,
As they roamed Colorado—but always they'd fail.

Till one day trudging east of the Great Divide
As they slithered and skid down a steep mountainside,
"Look yonder," shouts Whiskers, in words loud and bold,
"Right next to your feet lays a nugget of gold!"

So Valentine clutches the gold in his fist,
Recalling the fame and the fortune he'd missed,
While Whiskers in rage shouts, "It's plain as can be
That I spotted it first; this belongs now to me."

Vermont now insisted, "That just isn't so!"
(For gold drives men crazy, as you may well know).
They glared at each other in a moment of strife,
Vermont with his pistol, McCoy with his knife.

But before something happened to cause them both grief,
Old McCoy dropped his knife and breathed a sigh of relief;
"You're my friend, Valentine, and I can't run you through,
Not even for gold and so here's what we'll do:

"We can hike back to Denver beneath this full moon
And head straight for the Wandering Stranger saloon;
We'll play one hand of poker the very first night,
And it's winner take all—if you say that's all right."

"Agreed," said Vermont, "but one more thing I say,
So we're sure no one cheats in the game that we play,
We'll ask Beautiful Belle to sit down at our table
And deal out each card if she's willing and able."

7

"They glared at each other in a moment of strife,
Vermont with his pistol, McCoy with his knife."

Soon they sat down together with Belle in between,
Just cards and the nugget on a table of green;
"Five cards for you both," says Belle with a grin,
"Let's get this thing started and see who will win."

So they picked up their cards and gave a blank stare,
No sign of emotion to show what was there;
"Now, Vermont," says Old Whiskers, "I'm no different from you,
'Cause I'm holding three cards and I'm taking two."

The Beautiful Belle dealt each man a pair,
(You could hear a soft gasp from the crowd watching there);
And now the moment of truth was at hand,
Belle motioned to both, "Let's see where we stand."

"Vermont Valentine, now I'm throwing no bull,
I've got aces and eights and the house is full.
So beat 'em, my friend, with whatever you choose,
Beat 'em, my friend, or you're sure to lose."

Vermont fixed his eyes on the nugget of gold,
Then he flipped down his cards and just muttered, "I fold."
"I know when I'm beaten, Old Whiskers McCoy,
So the nugget is yours and I hope it brings joy."

The prospector clutched at his treasure of gold,
But now there's a twist as this story is told;
"To show I've no malice and still wish you well,
I'm giving this nugget to Beautiful Belle.

"For I value your friendship far more than my life,
Through good times or bad, through pleasure or strife;
'Twas only that nugget confusing my mind,
And the wilderness beckons to make a new find."

So they walked out together, back into the night;
(Two men who are friends make a wonderful sight!)
Old Whiskers McCoy and Vermont Valentine,
Still dreaming their dreams of a splendid gold mine.

"Without hesitation he swung wide the door."

2. Facing the Test

Down in Laredo this story is told,
How a man once was tested as fire tests gold;
Like so many heroes his deed now lies hid,
But I'll tell you the tale—and explain what he did:

"Those big Norton brothers were a hard riding pair,
When it came to the law, well, they didn't much care;
They were dirty, and strong, and awkward, and mean,
And to gamble at cards was their favorite routine.
"So one day they sat in the Red Hat Saloon,
Just drinkin' and sweatin' one hot afternoon,
When in came a-stumblin' Slim Jim McGunn
Who challenged them both to some poker—for fun.

"Now poker for fun is a risk I have learned,
Pretty soon Jim had lost every cent he had earned;
When all of a sudden he rose screaming, 'Fix!'
'Cause he counted those aces and found there were six.

"Jim stood up in rage though he lacked any gun,
Determined to finish what they had begun;
He accused them of cheating while dealing the hand—
And that's how Jim entered the Promised Land.

" 'Cause those big Norton brothers weren't much for a joke,
From their lightning fast six-guns came bullets and smoke;
'Next time,' they whispered, 'you be more discreet,
'Bout saying that Nortons were tryin' to cheat.'

"So those big Norton brothers had proved once again,
That they could shoot faster than most other men;
It wasn't the first time they'd settled with lead
The question of cheating—and three men were dead.

"Then they turned to Joe Bucket who stood by the door,
'Now listen here, Mister, you do us a chore;
You just tell that new sheriff we're waitin' for him
To see if he'll bother 'bout takin' us in.'

"As their messenger left they both roared with delight,
'Cause those Nortons were spoiling for just one more fight;
'I hope that new sheriff ain't gone very far,
It's time that he works so he earns that there star.'

"Young Sheriff Tom Cleet had begun to restore
To this rip-roaring town some semblance of law;
He wasn't the kind that would fill you with dread,
Yet everyone knew that he meant what he said.

"Still they wondered if it were just sheer fairy tale
When he said that he'd put both the Nortons in jail;
And though lots of folks would the Nortons disown,
Young Cleet had to walk down that street all alone.

"Tom knew that the Nortons were fast with a gun,
But it wouldn't be Cleet just to turn back and run;
That star on his chest meant that he was the law,
Is it backed up by steel—or only by straw?

"See everyone watch as he walks down the street,
Yes, everyone knows that he will not retreat;
Yet everyone fears that the Nortons will shoot,
And everyone's glad that it's just his dispute.

"As Tom walks down the street not a cowboy's in sight,
His heart pounds within and his face has turned white;
But there's no turning back till the job has been done,
Just one thing reassures—that's his loaded six-gun.

"Outside the saloon he calls out to the pair,
It's silent inside, but he knows someone's there;
'Whether dead or alive you're both going to jail,
And I'm stakin' my life that I'm not gonna fail.'

"As I told you before when this story began,
The sheriff now acted the part of a man;
Without hesitation he swung wide the door,
Hear the deafening noise as three six shooters roar.

"So you wonder what happened when blood had to flow?
Matter of fact, friend, you don't have to know;
'Cause a man's not a man just for coming out best,
But a man is a man—when he faces the test!"

"The hearts of men would melt when she would look them in the eye
And sing their favorite song of all, called 'Love Me 'Til I Die.'"

3. "Love Me 'Til I Die"

Up in northern Colorado near the border of the state,
Lies a quiet little ghost town that has long since met its fate;
The miners, and the cowpokes, and the Cheyenne long are gone,
But the tale of sweet Virginia Nash forever lingers on.

The town had sprung to life when silver mining once brought
     fame,
And men poured in from near and far so they might stake a claim;
But Tom Nash had a different plan to earn his fortune bright,
He opened up a tavern that was crowded every night.

Now Tom Nash had one daughter and Virginia was her name,
She had a golden singing voice that put the rest to shame;
When she sang a lively ballad how she thrilled those lonesome
     men,
Their cheers would bring the house down till she sang the song
     again.

Virginia knew the latest hits the New York people sing,
She'd belt them out and make a miner feel he was a king;
But when the clock passed midnight and the hour had grown old,
Virginia sang a haunting song shaped from a different mold.

For her voice became a whisper, like an angel she'd appear,
And the boisterous room grew silent as if judgement day were
     near;
The hearts of men would melt when she would look them in the
     eye
And sing their favorite song of all, called "Love Me 'Til I Die."

It's hard to say just why this song had magic from the start,
But "Love Me 'Til I Die" brought peace to every cowboy's heart;
And the miners all protested they would turn in all their cash,
Just to hear that lovely ballad sung by sweet Virginia Nash.

She had the opportunity to marry many men,
They discussed this with her father but they never settled when;
The proposals were rejected and the men would wonder why,
Still she haunted them each night by singing "Love Me 'Til I Die."

But now an air of mystery descends upon this tale,
For happy times have turned to sad and prayers now seem to fail.
The father searches up and down, confusion on his face,
For sweet Virginia Nash has disappeared without a trace.

Did Virginia go to Denver with some miner who was kind?
Or did she join that cowboy who had Texas on his mind?
Perhaps she dreamed of far New York where singing might bring
    fame,
She might be in Montana—or some other place you name.

Thirty years have passed so quickly and the mystery is not solved
To the grief and disappointment of most everyone involved;
Tom Nash is dead and buried but they still ask far and near,
"What happened to Virginia and the songs we loved to hear?"

By now the mines are empty, for the silver has run short,
But we'll always have the memories of the rowdy times it brought;
The miners started drifting seeking other sights and thrills,
And the village once so noisy is a ghost town in the hills.

Though people think a ghost town always is a lonely sight,
Still spirits from the past may roam and hover in the night;
The cowpokes and the miners once more utter with a sigh,
"Come back to us, Virginia, and sing 'Love Me 'Til I Die.' "

And the angels hear these spirits' prayer and yield to their request,
From across the far horizon comes the woman they love best;
She smiles at all their welcomes and greets them with a bow,
"Never mind my disappearance—for you see I'm with you now."

So join these misty spirits wandering in from different parts,
As they ask the fair Virginia Nash to sing and thrill their hearts;
And as the moon comes shining through the shadows of the sky,
Once more you'll hear Virginia whisper, "Love Me 'Til I Die."

4. The Memory of Blue

The "Walk In Saloon" was a-rockin' with noise,
There sat old Frankie Bly just amusing the boys
With his tale of that gal with the eyes of blue—
So pretend you are there, and he'll tell it to you:

"It was back in those days when the West seemed young,
If you rode into town, you would strap on your gun;
In this very saloon worked a lady I knew,
I've forgotten her name, but her eyes?—they were blue.

"In her red satin dress she would sing us some song,
Once she stopped by my table, yet not very long,
But for months after that as I rode on that range,
I saw eyes of blue—does it seem so strange?

"One night she argued with Big Tom McLarn,
That cowboy got rude and he twisted her arm,
And he'd twist it again, that was easy to see,
So I jumped from my place and said, 'Cowboy, try me!'

"Tom flung her aside as he turned his head,
If he went for his gun, well—I knew I was dead,
So I said to him fast before shootin' began,
'Take off the gunbelt and fight man to man.'

"Tom let out a roar you could hear near and far
As we both put our gunbelts on top of the bar;
With his size and his muscles, he needed no gun
And I thought to myself, 'Now what have I done?'

"As the lady in scarlet stood grateful nearby,
I saw once again the blue of her eye;
From the look on Tom's face there was no backin' down,
I must fight like a man or just clear out of town.

" 'Take off the gunbelt and fight man to man.' "

"Now the boys gathered round in an awkward shaped ring,
Next we stood toe to toe and began to swing;
Soon a punch to the forehead put me flat on the floor,
'Now, Mister,' he said, 'do you want any more?'

"So I got up again, do you want to know why?
Well—I looked at the gal, and she winked that blue eye,
And the onlookers tell me I did fairly well
But his fists were too strong and again I fell.

"I was stacked 'gainst the bar lying heels over head,
'It's all over now!' the proprietor said;
I was sick till I saw the blue of her eye,
Then I thought to myself, 'Just one more try.'

"But his punches of steel were too much to bear,
I flew over a table and smashed through a chair;
My nose now ran red and one eye was shut,
My shirt was all torn and my cheekbone was cut.

"As I got up I heard the gal utter a sigh,
And this time I saw—a tear in her eye;
It rolled down her cheek, guess I looked quite a sight—
Then the sheriff marched in and so ended the fight.

"So we paid up the bill for the things we had smashed,
Before we were through, six months' wages were cashed;
I was three days in bed and then back riding herd,
And that gal with blue eyes?—she had said not a word.

"It's been forty-five years since the night of that fight,
I know fightin's wrong, but I felt this was right;
McLarn went too far when he twisted her arm,
Just one man in that room could protect her from harm.

"Though I'm called the Old-Timer and have to walk slow,
How my thoughts carry back to that scene long ago;
Then I see once again—the blue of her eye,
And just think it was *me*—that caused her to sigh!"

"So Charlie was complying, but then Ringo disagreed,
He aimed his trusty shotgun and said, 'This is all you'll need.'"

5. The Ace of Spades

They tell of Charles McKenna who was balding, slow and fat,
Who wore an ace of spades stuck in the band around his hat;
Still he drove the Arizona stage with confidence and grace
And welcomed all the world with one big smile upon his face.

Bart Ringo was his partner and rode shotgun on each trip
With a faithful loaded six-gun strapped on tightly to his hip;
He was handsome, he was sturdy, he had muscles made of steel,
He had everything that Charlie lacked for feminine appeal.

But the two men formed a friendship that grew stronger on the
    trail,
As the stagecoach hauled its passengers, plus payroll, and some
    mail;
Bart Ringo was the envy of the local fair young maids,
While Charlie wore a hat that flashed his lucky ace of spades.

Five years they rode together as they sat atop the stage,
The pair were known as partners who worked hard to earn their
    wage;
But then one day in Tucson, Ringo broke some sudden news:
"Next month I'm getting married to the dark-haired Kathy
    Hughes."

So Charlie was delighted that his friend had found a wife,
But that very night in Tucson a surprise now changed his life;
Buster Hancock was found murdered in an alley on his face,
And on the ground next to the corpse they found an upturned ace.

So the sheriff said to Charlie just as quickly as could be:
"You're the man whose hat holds aces, and you'll have to come
    with me."
But Ringo told the sheriff, "Why, you surely have no case,
To blame this crime on Charlie just because you found an ace."

21

But that's just the way it happened, for the jury did not fail,
By circumstantial evidence, poor Charlie went to jail;
Bart Ringo was heartbroken, there was anger on his face,
To think they'd send his friend to jail based on an upturned ace.

Bart kept in touch with Charlie and one day he wrote the news:
"It's not the same without you, but I've married Kathy Hughes."
Ten years moved on so slowly, prison life can take its toll,
But finally Charlie was released, sent out upon parole.

He headed back to Tucson and told Ringo right away:
"If I can drive that stage again, I'll work for any pay;
I still can be your partner if you'll lend a helping hand,
When it comes to driving horses, I'm the best man in the land."

Now Ringo had connections and he soon arranged it so
That he and Charlie worked the stage, the same as long ago;
And as Charlie drove the stagecoach with an ace stuck in his hat,
He once again was smiling and he still was bald and fat.

Till that morning west of Tucson when a bandit hove in sight,
"Just hand me down that payroll and there won't be any fight."
So Charlie was complying, but then Ringo disagreed,
He aimed his trusty shotgun and said, "This is all you'll need."

Next Ringo pulled the trigger, but the bandit fired too,
And Ringo dropped upon the ground—as dying men will do;
The outlaw grabbed the payroll next, but Charlie drew his gun
And stopped that bandit in his tracks before the deed was done.

Then Charlie turned to Ringo and asked what he could do,
But Ringo said, "The way I feel, I know my life is through;
But I've got a secret, Charlie, that's for you and me to share,
Because when a man is dying, well, he wants to clear the air.

"You remember Buster Hancock and that murder long ago?
You always claimed your innocence and, yes, I know it's so;
It was me who murdered Hancock, so as not to leave a trace,
Before I fled that alley, I left on the ground an ace.

"I thought you'd have an alibi and surely would go free,
I thought they'd all be so confused, they'd never think of me;
My heart was set on Kathy Hughes and marrying that gal,
And so I could achieve this, I betrayed you, faithful pal.

"But now I want to clear your name by telling one and all,
That Charlie's surely innocent, for me he took the fall;
So quickly write a paper that explains this awful crime,
And before I met my Maker, that's the last thing I will sign."

But Charlie smiled at Ringo who had little time to live,
And told him, "All I want to say is, 'Partner, I forgive.'
I'll never share this secret with the townsfolk or your wife,
We're partners to the bitter end, through good times and through
        strife."

So Ringo was a hero as he went into the grave,
And Charlie knew his secret would a reputation save;
It's true they still say Charlie killed a man and went to jail,
But when two men are partners, then their friendship cannot fail.

So here's to Charlie McKenna who is old, and bald, and fat,
Who wears an ace of spades stuck in the wide band of his hat;
That ace once caused some trouble, but he gladly took the fall,
His partner's lying in the grave—a hero to us all.

"He pulled out his gun as the wind now grew still."

6. Legend of the Northwest

Up north of the Yukon in the days of old,
Where all kinds of adventurers panned for gold,
Legends were told of the men who brought peace,
The men of the Northwest Mounted Police.

It was said in that land where the husky ran
That a Mountie will always get his man,
And that legend lives on till this very day,
Let me tell you a story to prove what I say:

There was a fight one night at the Big Moose Mine,
(The boys had been drinking—and I don't mean wine!)
Bill Park got so mad that he lost his head;
He pulled out a Colt and shot Clark full of lead.

Then he aimed at the foreman and said real slow,
"Better give me that payroll before I go";
He hitched up some dogs and took off down the trail,
And here's where the Mountie comes into the tale.

One man now dead and the town in a frenzy,
When into the camp rode the Mountie Mackenzie;
First he heard of Park's crime and then learned of his route,
With a sled and his dogs he took off in pursuit.

"Mush!" he roared out to the dogs one and all,
As the crisp winter snow quickly started to fall;
He thought to himself as he drove down the trail,
"I'll catch him by dark—if the huskies don't fail."

So on went the chase as the snow and wind howled,
While the bull moose sought shelter and the wolf pack prowled;
The Sergeant grew worried as it quickly grew dark,
He turned one more bend—and there stood Bill Park.

"Hey, Mountie," he called from behind a pine tree,
"I'll kill once again if you won't let me be;
I've got you covered with my Colt .45,
Turn back on the trail—if you like being alive."

"Bill Park," called Mackenzie, "you know you can't win,
Because whatever you threaten, I'm taking you in."
He pulled out his gun as the wind now grew still,
Without further talk he advanced towards Bill.

The trapped outlaw crouched and then fired his gun,
He gave a cruel laugh though he knew what he'd done;
The officer staggered—then shot back at his foe,
Park cried out in rage as he fell in the snow.

Mackenzie could see that his man was not dead,
Despite his own wound he dragged Park to the sled;
Back for the payroll—each step caused him pain,
While the crisp winter snow had now changed into rain.

Three hours later, Mackenzie came in,
"Hooray," roared the miners, "we knew Mac would win."
The dogs dashed down Main Street to the tune of the lash,
"Here's your man," cried Mackenzie and next threw them the
    cash.

So here's to Mackenzie—as brave as they come,
The Mountie whose work is finally done;
He followed the trail to wherever it led,
He brought in his man, and then fell over—dead!

7. Dangerous Blue

There was a horse in Colorado that they used to just call "Blue,"
But he threw so many riders that they called him "dangerous" too;
He was the wildest bucking bronco that the West had ever seen,
So Dangerous Blue grew famous from Cheyenne to Abilene.

Fifty riders tried to break him and submit him to their will,
Fifty riders all went flying and the horse was champion still;
And so the claim went forth and all agreed that it was true:
There's not a cowpoke in the West can conquer Dangerous Blue.

So they threw a lasso round the horse and settled on a test,
The great Durango rodeo will prove which man is best;
"We will pay one thousand dollars, this is only fit and due,
To the man who spends twelve seconds on the back of Dangerous
     Blue."

You'd expect one hundred cowboys would come forth to stake a
     claim,
But Dangerous Blue, the stallion, was so fearsome in his fame
That they only found three riders who would make this boast to
     you:
"I can spend a full twelve seconds on the back of Dangerous Blue."

Charlie Johnson from New Mexico was always strong and rough,
He told folks in Durango, "I'll just call that horse's bluff,
And if I win that money, then there's one thing you can bet,
There'll be a party in Durango no one ever will forget."

Billy Parker came from Texas to Wyoming's rolling hills,
If he rode the horse twelve seconds, first he had to pay some bills;
"Then I'm heading back to Dallas just as quickly as can be
'Cause a gal I know there's waiting for nobody else but me."

Little Luke McDonough had a ranch not far from town,
The heavy mortgage on his spread would sometimes get him
     down;
"If I ride that horse twelve seconds, using all my craft and guile,
Then my problems will be over and the wife and kids can smile."

"The wildest bucking bronco from Cheyenne to Abilene."

Now they had a special system to determine who had won,
Old Judge Mathias Turner sat with timepiece and a gun;
He'd count off twelve slow seconds, if a rider still was there,
Then he'd raise his trusty six-gun, shoot a bullet in the air.

Next the cowboys drew a straw, which was the way they would
      decide
On who was the lucky cowboy who would be the first to ride;
Billy Parker drew the long straw and was told, "It's up to you
To be the first one ever to outhustle Dangerous Blue."

So Billy straddles Dangerous Blue and eases on real slow,
He wraps the reins around his fist and calls out, "Let him go!"
They open up the gate and Dangerous Blue is free and mean,
The wildest bucking bronco from Cheyenne to Abilene.

The seconds seem like hours, horse and rider everywhere,
Judge Turner eyes his timepiece with his six-gun in the air;
Parker thinks of home in Texas where that gal still loves him true,
But now he's twisting in the air, the victim of old Blue.

The people of Durango all let out a rousing cheer,
The horse is still the master of the man this day it's clear;
And now it's Charlie Johnson's turn to see what he can do,
He creeps into the saddle on the top of Dangerous Blue.

The horse is spitting fire as he hurtles through the air,
The mighty law of gravity soon separates the pair;
So there won't be any party, Charlie's headfirst on the ground,
His unseating came so fast that not a person makes a sound.

Number three is Luke McDonough with the mortgage on his
      mind,
He's stayed on all the horses any rodeo could find;
But now he's met his match and Dangerous Blue is in command,
Judge Turner reaches nine when Luke is tasting dust and sand.

As Dangerous Blue stands all alone at center of the ring,
The natives of Durango know this horse is still the king;
The judge puts his revolver in its holster once again,
He's timed this horse so many times—but never got past ten.

When cowboys get together 'cause some rodeo's due to meet,
Here's what they tell each other in saloons and on the street:
"You can try your roping cattle or whatever else they do,
But the greatest thrill a rodeo has—is riding Dangerous Blue."

And when people in Durango talk of horses they have seen,
They know which one's the wildest from Cheyenne to Abilene;
Some say it's just a legend, others pledge their word it's true:
There has never been a man on earth, could stay on Dangerous
    Blue.

8. The Double Hanging

There's a legend that they'll tell you where the Pecos River flows,
How they had a double hanging and how no one really knows
If it was Robby Halpen or if it was Rodney Sloth
Who murdered Tim McPhee—or does the guilt belong to both?

Robby Halpen hailed from Georgia, came to Texas as a boy,
Earned his living roping cattle and his life became a joy
When he met the gentle Mary Kane with eyes of palest blue,
He said one day he'd marry her, she promised to be true.

Another cowboy Rodney Sloth was Halpen's closest friend,
He was known to have a temper and a will that would not bend;
Still Halpen stood beside him and the other cowboys knew
You couldn't fight just one of them, you'd have to fight the two.

One Friday night they rode to town despite a heavy rain,
While Rodney played some poker, Halpen looked for Mary Kane;
He found her with one blue eye shut, her pain was clear to see,
She said she had a run-in with that gambler Tim McPhee.

So Robby's face grew angry and he said, "I won't take long
To make quite sure that Tim McPhee will sing a different song."
Mary answered, "Don't be foolish, for I only ask from you
That wherever you may wander, you will still see eyes of blue."

But Robby Halpen's mind was set, he went to the saloon
Where Rodney and McPhee now sat alone in the back room;
A poker game was under way, the chips were all piled high
In front of Tim McPhee while Rodney Sloth sat wondering why.

But now a dread catastrophe descends upon the room:
The three men sat there all alone in early morning gloom,
When suddenly two shots ring out, the bullets find their goal,
And Tim McPhee falls to the floor—may heaven rest his soul.

31

"Next Sloth and Halpen both affirm, 'This wasn't done by me.' "

Soon Sheriff Douglas is on hand to check upon the pair,
Their guns are fully loaded and they give an empty stare;
Next Sloth and Halpen both affirm, "This wasn't done by me."
Just one man might reveal the truth—that's poor dead Tim
    McPhee.

First Rodney Sloth tells Douglas, "I was only sitting here,
When angry Robby Halpen came upon us from the rear;
He challenged Tim McPhee and said, 'You injured Mary Kane,'
Before I knew what happened, why that gambler had been slain."

But Halpen still protested that he didn't do the crime:
"It's true I had a motive and McPhee is only slime;
But he and Rodney came to blows about the poker game,
If I were never in the room, things still would be the same."

And next the blue-eyed Mary Kane came rushing to the room,
She saw the stricken victim and men's faces streaked with gloom:
"Oh, tell me, Robby Halpen, did you shoot down Tim McPhee?
But still I trust you're innocent so wait, please wait, for me."

There now arose a fierce debate about the ugly crime,
The wisdom of King Solomon was needed at this time;
But no one really could decide which one should get the noose,
If they knew who was guilty, they would turn the other loose.

Next up spoke Peter Hatchet with a theory quite unique:
"The two of them are guilty and it's both of them we seek;
They're trying to confuse us all by passing on the blame,
If we let either man escape, we'll hang our heads in shame."

And so a disagreement raged among the angry men
In deciding who was guilty, finally Hatchet spoke again:
"The more I think about it, this appears a certain fact
That both these men are guilty and it's time for us to act."

Next they threw a pair of lassos round the limb of an oak tree,
Then Sheriff Douglas slowly said, "I guess we all agree
That both men had a motive and are guilty in our sight
Of gunning down McPhee—and so to hang them is our right."

So they held a double hanging as the morning sun did shine,
While standing near, sweet Mary Kane was heard to softly pine:
"Are you guilty, Robby Halpen, did you murder Tim McPhee?
But still I trust you're innocent, so wait, please wait, for me."

So the men of Pecos, Texas, still this story do relate,
How there was a double hanging and two cowboys met their fate,
And of how blue-eyed Mary Kane was torn apart inside,
Protesting Halpen's innocence until the day she died.

So, partner, since you know the facts as they did long ago,
Now won't you be the final judge and promptly let us know:
"Would you hold a double hanging as the townsfolk did agree?
Or would you string up neither one—and set the two men free?"

9. The Last Bullet

There's a town lies west of Denver and it sits atop some gold,
So the miners formed a company and now the story's told
How they piled up all their nuggets in a sack of gold one day,
How they planned to sell the gold and get some dollars for their
pay.

"We need someone we can trust to cart away this loaded sack,
To sell our gold in Denver, get the cash, and hurry back;
Now the men are getting restless for the wages they deserve,
Does anybody know a man who's honest and has nerve?"

"There's a cowboy working back in town, his name is Thomas
Shea,
He used to be a sheriff, you can trust him they all say;
He's handy with a six-gun and the best of all our men
To get this gold to Denver and return to us again."

So they found this quiet cowboy, quickly told him of his task:
"Can you cart some gold to Denver, do this favor that we ask?
If you bring the miner's payroll back to town by Saturday,
You'll receive one hundred dollars, are you with us, Thomas
Shea?"

And so Thomas picked the sack up and then to the miners said:
"If I don't bring back your payroll, you can figure that I'm dead."
Soon he climbed aboard the train, for distant Denver he was
bound,
The trip should take five hours if no trouble would be found.

But gold brings out the worst in men, I think you may agree,
It captivates some cutthroat's heart who dreams of what might be;
And so four miners boldly schemed, "This gold is ours today,
If we can only stop that train and hold up Thomas Shea."

35

"Soon it was only Thomas Shea crouched low inside the car."

They loaded up their pistols and then picked a lonely spot
Where they stacked up boulders on the track to hatch their wicked
    plot:
"The train will stop and everyone will do just as they're told,
Including Thomas Shea, who'll quickly yield his sack of gold."

And so the train came to a halt, each outlaw aimed his gun,
The passengers all scurried off, the holdup had begun;
Soon it was only Thomas Shea crouched low inside the car,
The miner-bandits told themselves, "It's going well so far."

They knew that Shea was still inside though he lay out of view,
Zeke Webster shouted, "Listen, friend, I tell you what we'll do:
Just drop that sack of gold right out the window, like we say,
You'll live to see tomorrow and we'll soon be on our way."

Shea clutched his gun, stretched on the floor, and then he boldly
    said:
"The only way you'll get this gold is first to shoot me dead.
So if you really want it and we can't seem to agree,
Then come inside and get it—if you care to deal with me."

A gunfight now erupted as the bandits sought a way
To get their golden treasure and to put an end to Shea;
The passengers stood near the train, unsure of who would win,
And Thomas Shea fought all alone, refusing to give in.

At last the guns grew silent and so now the outlaws knew
It was time to climb aboard the train and do what they must do;
So Spider Parker leaped inside to meet with sudden strife,
A bullet from the gun of Shea deprived him of his life.

Then Roscoe Morgan came on next, a pistol in his hand,
But Shea returned his fire, sent him to the Promised Land;
Of four men in the outlaw band, there now lived only two,
They hesitated briefly as they wondered what to do.

As Thomas Shea fought for his life, he suddenly grew cold,
He only had one bullet left to save his sack of gold;
And soon the Webster brothers grasped the trouble he was in,
"He's hiding in there somewhere and his ammo's running thin.

"His gun may now be empty or perhaps the fellow's dead."
Now sensing that the kill was near, one Webster brother said:
"We know you're out of bullets or you'd surely fire back,
So what's the use of dying, why not throw us out the sack?"

Then Shea returned this answer, "Yes, I must admit it's true,
That I'm down to my last bullet if that's any news to you;
So climb aboard together if you dare to be so bold,
Then one of you will bite the dust—and one will get the gold."

And so the Webster brothers looked each other in the eye,
"Is it really worth a sack of gold for one of us to die?"
With two men dead they realized this was not their lucky day,
They climbed upon their horses and they made their getaway.

Four hours later and the train pulled into Denver town,
The tales of all the passengers brought Shea his just renown;
"Is it really true you only had a single bullet more
To keep that pair of outlaw men from settling the score?"

"When I was in that awful bind, I thought of what I'd said,
That I'd protect this sack of gold until they found me dead;
And so I called those outlaws' bluff and to myself was true,
When you're down to your last bullet—that's the only thing to
     do."

10. To Look Death in the Eye

One day in San Francisco just a century ago,
A man named Pepper Carney met his nephew Bucky Coe;
The boy was only twelve and yet an orphan lad was he,
For his parents, dead from typhoid, had been buried out at sea.

So Pepper had a problem: how to help his youthful kin,
For he knew just to forget the boy would be an awful sin;
But Pepper also had a dream to make his fortune bold,
He would head up to the Yukon and, with luck, discover gold.

So he sat down next to Bucky and said, "Son, let me be frank,
I'm just a rough and tumble guy—no money in the bank;
But they say up in the Yukon there is gold at every turn,
Still it's awfully hard to find it—but a man can surely learn.

"I'll be heading for the Yukon and I'm set to pan for gold,
So you're welcome, lad, to join me if your heart is brave and bold;
You're mighty young to make this trip, but what else can we do?
I used to travel all alone—but now it's me and you."

So Bucky said to Pepper, "Tell me how to be a man."
The uncle answered slowly, "Learn this lesson if you can:
Sometimes a fellow doubts if he will live or he will die,
If trouble comes, it takes a man to look death in the eye."

So they hopped a ship and headed north to Skagway on the coast,
"We'll come home with a fortune," was what everyone would
      boast;
By now the Get-Rich-Fever had grasped Pepper in its hold,
"It's along the Yukon River that we'll surely find some gold."

There's a town upon the Yukon and Dawson is its name,
Soon Pepper said to Bucky, "That's the place we'll strike a claim."
So they headed north to Dawson set to pay fierce winter's cost,
When a blizzard caught them on the trail and soon they both were
      lost.

"And so the pair went loping on with torches in the air."

"Unless this storm lets up real fast, we'll perish in the snow."
Next Pepper growled at Bucky, "Here's the law you've got to
    know:
Sometimes a fellow doubts if he will live or he will die,
If trouble comes, it takes a man to look death in the eye."

Just when it seemed the Specter Death would now come passing
    by,
Fair Providence stepped in and said, "It's not your turn to die."
For they stumbled on a cabin, warmth and shelter it would give,
Soon they started up a fire and how good it was to live.

So Pepper said to Bucky, "What a fool I've grown to be,
You should be back in Frisco and not freezing next to me."
But now the spirit of the north had Bucky in its hold,
"Let's reach the Yukon, Pepper, and I know we'll strike some gold.

"I don't want to be a burden, I just want to be a man,
And I know I'm tougher, stronger than the day when we began;
As long as I can be with you, I'll live or I can die,
When we struggled through that blizzard, I looked death straight
    in the eye."

So they trudged ahead to Dawson facing challenges so bold,
Where they built a little cabin that was drafty, small and cold;
But late one afternoon as they brought in some firewood,
To their surprise a pack of wolves surrounded where they stood.

Pepper Carney had a six-gun, but for bullets only three,
He ordered Bucky not to run—"Just stay real close to me."
The cabin was a mile away and safety lay inside,
The woods were covered deep with snow without a place to hide.

But Bucky grabbed his flannel shirt and ripped it clean in two,
Wrapped the pieces round some branches and said, "This is what
    we'll do:
I'll light these flannel patches, we'll have torches as we run,
We'll head straight for the cabin, if they charge us, use your gun."

And so the pair went loping on with torches in the air,
While hungry wolves would snarl and growl around the
    frightened pair;
They used handkerchiefs and Pepper's shirt to keep the flames
    alive;
Each sprinted quickly 'cross the snow determined to survive.

And when they locked that cabin door, their hearts were filled
    with joy,
Then Pepper looked at Bucky and he whispered to the boy:
"Sometimes a fellow doubts if he will live or he will die,
If trouble comes, it takes a man to look death in the eye."

You've heard of all those men who left the Yukon without gold?
Well, that's not the way it happened as this story now is told;
For Bucky and his uncle struck it rich one summer's day,
They packed the gold into a bag and headed on their way.

Back south across the wilderness till Skagway came in sight,
Good luck was theirs, a ship for home would leave that very night.
Soon San Francisco's Golden Gate its welcome did provide,
But as they left the ship, a stranger stepped up to their side.

"I've heard you fellows found some gold along the Yukon's shore,
But here in San Francisco, you won't need it any more;
'Cause now I've got this gun that says, 'Just give that gold to me.'
It's easy come and easy go—my friends, don't you agree?"

Old Pepper glared in anger and said, "This is what I've got."
He pulled his gun and fired while the stranger also shot;
But at that very instant Bucky jumped between the pair,
The stranger's bullet struck his chest, he fell and gasped for air.

Two figures lay upon the ground, a man and just a lad,
Old Pepper propped up Bucky and said, "Well, we've just been
    had.
I took you to the Yukon so that we could partners be,
But now I'd give up all this gold to see you smile at me."

So Bucky said to Pepper as he lay upon the ground,
"Remember that it's not just gold the two of us have found;
There's a law of human living and you've taught it to me straight,
So whatever happens to me now, I'm ready for my fate.

"So here's the lesson, Pepper, that you've taught me oh so well,
The lesson that I'm needing now—as anyone can tell:
Sometimes a fellow doubts if he will live or he will die,
If trouble comes, it takes a man to look death in the eye."

"Then take a chance and ride the famous stagecoach to Cheyenne."

11. Stagecoach to Cheyenne

When a stranger comes to Denver and excitement is his plan,
There's a piece of fond advice we always proffer to the man;
You may share some bold experience you'll never see again,
If you take a chance and ride the famous stagecoach to Cheyenne.

The town's north across the border in Wyoming's rolling hills
And the characters who travel there can bring a stack of thrills;
Let me talk about some people who may join you now and then,
If you take a chance and ride the famous stagecoach to Cheyenne.

Willie Piper was a cowpoke years ago, the story's told,
But he headed straight for Denver when his friends discovered
    gold;
Now Willie's disillusioned with those dreams of gold he had,
He's decided herding cattle back in Cheyenne's not so bad.

Thomas Wilson is the driver, all the passengers agree
That he leads three pairs of horses as expertly as can be;
Buffalo or desperadoes—they just liven up the day,
 For he loves to find adventure as a way to earn his pay.

Riding shotgun on the stagecoach is a man they just call Sled,
Had an argument in Dallas where he left two fellows dead;
But now he's far from Texas and he earns an honest wage,
While carrying a rifle to protect the Cheyenne stage.

We remember last October when the stage drove out of town,
The brothers Mason ambushed her with six-guns and a frown;
They cleaned out all the passengers and just to make things clear,
Put a bullet in Sled's shoulder when he tried to interfere.

As you travel north from Denver, there are mountains to the west,
But soon the Rockies disappear, you'll pull up for a rest;
Then it's on again past sunset as you race for far Cheyenne,
All the travelers have a reason why they're leaving where they've
    been.

Philip Randall makes a living by selecting real estate,
But he's different from the others 'cause he loves to speculate;
He's heard they'll build a railroad soon from Denver to Cheyenne,
So he's riding north with dreams to earn a fortune once again.

Behind those rolling hills a band of Cheyenne may now wait,
The unsuspecting passengers could face a bloody fate;
For the riders might come charging to correct the wrongs at hand,
In a way, I understand them 'cause I guess they own this land.

Peg O'Brien's father never cared much for Buck Ray,
He thought the man lacked character and sent him on his way;
But Peggy says she loves him, full of eagerness and pride,
If she finds Buck in Cheyenne, she vows to stay and be his bride.

You'll see herds of giant bison as you travel through the day,
If they cross the trail in front of you, there'll be a big delay;
We love to hunt the buffalo for meat that is the best,
Some say they'll one day vanish as the settlers drive on west.

Charles Dillon is a gambler with a mustache sleek and trim,
He reached Denver from Chicago, but bad luck still follows him;
So now it's off to Cheyenne or some other distant port,
He thought he'd won the pot, but ended up ten thousand short.

Robert Smith's a politician and for Washington he's bound,
But to win a close election is quite difficult, he's found;
Last November back in Denver he was beaten once again,
But a good man never quits—and so he'll try now in Cheyenne.

The stage is coming round the bend, the hoofbeats we can hear,
The citizens of Cheyenne now let out a mighty cheer;
Tom Wilson's in the driver's seat assuring every soul
That the trip to here from Denver is just like a friendly stroll.

So here's to all those travelers riding boldly 'cross the West,
With all their faults they've made this land, America, the best;
If you seek the opportunity to be where men are men,
Then take a chance and ride the famous stagecoach to Cheyenne.

12. Cold Blue Eyes of Steel

Do you miss the thrills of yesteryear when cowboys rode the
    range?
When strapping on a six-gun was more commonplace than
    strange;
Let me tell you now the story of a man named Rex McNeil
Who became a Texas legend with his cold blue eyes of steel.

When the Civil War had ended, Dallas, Texas, rose to fame
As the wildest, toughest cattle town that anyone could name;
So the townsfolk all protested that a sheriff must be found
To rein in all those cowboys—some man who'll stand his ground.

So they had a civic meeting, all the citizens were there,
They were making little progress till one rancher did declare:
"To be our town's first sheriff, there's one man who'd be ideal,
He's working at the Stallion Ranch, his name is Rex McNeil."

Now Rex McNeil stood straight and tall, a man of iron will,
Well known for bustin' broncos, which was Rex's greatest skill;
He was handy with a six-gun and he said he'd give a try,
When the townsfolk all assured him, "You're our sheriff till you
    die."

The reason they elected Rex was not for style or grace,
But rather for the firm, hard look one saw upon his face;
The hearts of men would skip a beat, uneasy they would feel,
When Rex McNeil looked through them with his cold blue eyes of
    steel.

One night at Murphy's Grand Saloon, they held a poker game,
The six men round the able were the roughest you could name;
Tom Price was losing money and he challenged Roscoe Beck:
"Those last two cards you dealt came from the bottom of the
    deck."

"Then he muttered to the sheriff, 'Reckon I'll go back with you.' "

So it seemed an altercation was all set now to begin,
'Cause when the chips are stacked so high, a man might cheat to
     win;
Tom Price next drew his six-gun as the court of last appeal,
He looked up from the table—there stood steel-eyed Rex McNeil.

"Now, men, I'll only say this once, here's how it's going to be:
We're starting off this hand again, the dealer will be me."
Rex glanced around the table with his cold blue eyes of steel,
No man raised an objection so he now began to deal.

The six men round the table bet, based on the hand they'd got,
And as Lady Luck would have it, Tom Price won the giant pot;
With piercing eyes on every man, the sheriff took his stand:
"And now this game is over, friends, that was the final hand."

They tell of how Bill Ford once stole some other cowboy's horse,
And so it fell to Rex McNeil to bring him back, of course;
They met along the river thirty miles on down the trail,
Rex said, "I want that horse back and you must spend time in jail."

Bill Ford had other notions with a six-gun at his side,
Should he draw his gun or just give in, he now had to decide;
He looked into the sheriff's face, but all it would reveal
Was the firm determination of those cold blue eyes of steel.

The horse thief stared one minute at those icy eyes of blue,
Then he muttered to the sheriff, "Reckon I'll go back with you."
The outlaw probably figured that a shootout was not wise,
When he saw that look of coldness in the sheriff's steel blue eyes.
One year the town's best gossips had some news that they could
     leak,
That Rex McNeil and Lilly Drew would marry the next week;
Most folks were flabbergasted that the wedding bells would peal
For the man who'd grown so famous with his cold blue eyes of
     steel.

And so the two were married, Lilly now was Rex's wife,
Although she knew a sheriff's job was not the safest life;
You can picture in your daydreams all the charms of Lilly Drew,
The only sight on earth could melt those steely eyes of blue.

One night the town was crowded just before a cattle drive,
And two cowboys both were boasting, "I'm the fastest gun alive."
So they held a competition just to prove what they had said,
Both drew their guns and fired and soon one of them was dead.

So now the sheriff had to prove he could control this town,
He firmly said, "You've killed a man, now lay that handgun
    down."
But the killer would have none of this, he said, "So you're the law?
Well, now's your chance to prove it," and he challenged Rex to
    draw.

The pair stood twenty feet apart and each man fired his gun,
The killer tumbled to the ground and so McNeil had won;
Sometimes you've got to show a man the words you say are real,
Sometimes a job just can't be done with only eyes of steel.

So here's your invitation, come to Dallas any day,
Ride in to check out for yourself the truth of what I say;
And when you gallop in some time, I wonder how you'll feel,
When Rex McNeil looks through you—with his cold blue eyes of
    steel.

13. To Flip a Coin

Long ago in Sacramento, two Pike brothers owned some land,
But they both felt very restless and each had a plan at hand:
"Let's move to San Francisco," pleaded Stephen every day,
But Billy said, "New Mexico is where we ought to stay."

So the brothers found a system that would keep their friendship
    true,
Pulling out a silver dollar, Stephen said, "Here's what we'll do:
I'll flip this coin high in the air, this always does the trick,
You call it out, it's head or tails, the winner gets his pick."

So Billy called out tails and this prediction turned out true,
And soon it was New Mexico the brothers headed to;
Stephen wanted Albuquerque, Billy dreamed of Santa Fe,
So they flipped that silver dollar, once more Billy had his way.

Five years they herded cattle and worked odd jobs they could find,
Stephen's dreams of San Francisco had now vanished from his
    mind;
The brothers loved New Mexico and filling out life's joy,
Both Bill and brother Stephen fell for blonde-haired Kate McCoy.

So Stephen said to Billy, "To each other let's be true,
We can't let Kate divide us with her lovely eyes of blue;
Now one of us must court her, and one must step aside,
It's best that only one of us ask Kate to be his bride."

Next Billy asked his brother, "Can we settle this today?"
And Stephen had the answer for this problem right away:
"I'll flip this silver dollar in the air with one great hurl,
You call it out, it's heads or tails, the winner gets the girl."

So Billy had a wedding, Kate McCoy became his bride,
And now you may be thinking: What a strange way to decide;
But Bill and Kate were happy, and for sons she bore him two,
And, yes, the brothers' friendship still ran wide, and deep, and
    true.

"Quick as a flash Steve shot his gun and hit the falling coin."

If a cowboy can improve himself, he's looking for the chance,
To be the town's lone sheriff is one fast way to advance;
When Stephen was elected, he told Bill without delay,
"I want you to be my deputy, we'll shake up Santa Fe."

So Stephen served as sheriff, brother Billy at his side,
The brothers Pike grew famous all across the countryside;
"They run an honest town," is what the people used to say,
But their chance to prove their mettle had to come on one hot day.

That marauder Tom McCall came riding straight into the bank,
With six-guns drawn, he shouted out, "Now listen, I'll be frank;
Either fill my saddle bags with all the money that you've got,
Or they'll bury you at sunset in a six-foot sandy plot."

As Tom McCall rode out the door, he fired from his horse,
Next Steve and Billy Pike now had to make their move, of course;
They sprung into the saddle to bring justice to McCall,
But fate stepped in, the outlaw's horse then tripped and took a fall.

Tom leaped up in an instant, his saddle bags in hand
And headed for the stable as a place to make his stand;
While Steve and Billy Pike assured each other without doubt,
"He's trapped inside the stable and we've got to flush him out."

So Billy said to Stephen, "Now this time we must agree
That I go in straight after him, you stay and cover me."
But Stephen said to Billy, "You've got two kids and a wife,
To stop a rascal like McCoy is just not worth your life."

So there was a disagreement on the matter now at hand,
But Stephen's silver dollar brings solutions on demand:
"I'll flip this coin high in the air, this always does the trick,
You call it out, it's heads or tails, the winner gets his pick."

But love and friendship now prevailed, the bonds that brothers
    join,
Quick as a flash Steve shot his gun and hit the falling coin;
"You have a way of knowing what this coin is going to say,
So to blazes with that dollar 'cause I'm going in today."

And that's the way it happened, Stephen just presumed he'd won,
He walked into the stable where the outlaw held his gun;
A sudden confrontation, shots were fired instantly,
Then silence fell upon the land while Billy went to see.

McCall lay on his deathbed and a gloom now filled the place,
For Stephen too was dying though a smile shone on his face;
"You tell your blue-eyed Kate that now she has to care for you,
There's no use flipping coins when duty tells you what to do.

"But I know you've stood beside me in the choices that we've
    made,
If we went to San Francisco, I might not have made the grade."
Billy saw his brother fading and he wondered what to do,
To prove one final time his love ran wide, and deep, and true.

"If only *we* could judge if you will live or you will die."
"Imagine that we had the chance," said Stephen with a sigh:
"I'll flip a coin high in the air, this always does the trick,
You call it out, it's heads or tails, the winner gets his pick."

14. A Gal Called Dallas Blue

All those cowboys down in Dallas tell a tale of long ago,
Though some of them will argue how the story ought to go;
Let me tell you of a cowpoke by the name of Bobby Kean,
And of a gal who had the bluest eyes you've ever seen.

Bobby Kean grew up in Dallas working on his father's range,
He had a single sweetheart and his mind would never change;
She grew up on a nearby ranch with eyes of purest blue,
And she rode a snow-white stallion the way no one else could do.

I don't recall the gal's real name, in fact, I just don't care,
But she had the sweetest, bluest eyes that made those cowboys
      stare;
The men rode in from far and near to check if she were true,
And because she had such lovely eyes, they called her Dallas Blue.

She had her choice of many men and suitors by the score,
She'd smile at them with eyes of blue, and some men's hopes
      would soar;
But Dallas Blue would gently say, "Of all the men I've seen,
The only one appeals to me is Cowboy Bobby Kean."

So Bobby Kean and Dallas Blue become a local pair,
She rode her snow-white stallion and they never had a care;
Bobby said, "We'll soon be married, for my heart belongs to you,"
As he gazed into the haunting eyes of lovely Dallas Blue.

But Dallas' father formed the grandest plan you've ever seen,
He organized a cattle drive straight up to Abilene;
Bobby Kean joined with the others driving north to sell the herd,
When Dallas Blue came riding up to greet him with this word:

"You'll reach the wide Red River in a week if you take care,
So look across the river, waiting for you, I'll be there;
I'll be waving from my snow-white horse and hoping to be seen,
To show how much I love you and I need you, Bobby Kean."

" 'I'll be waving from my snow-white horse and hoping to be seen,
To show how much I love you and I need you, Bobby Kean.' "

So Bobby was delighted as he gazed at Dallas Blue,
And when he saw those haunting eyes, he knew just what to do;
He kissed her once and whispered, "Think about me now and
    then,
Till we meet at the Red River and I'll be at peace again."

So the cattle drive went moving north, but as they crossed the
    plain,
As luck would have it, they were plagued with five straight days
    of rain;
And so the fierce Red River was a torrent on that day,
To get the herd across would make those ranch hands earn their
    pay.

As the cowboys led the cattle to cross that river wide,
They saw a woman waving at them from the other side;
They really couldn't say how Dallas Blue had got across,
But she plunged into the river set atop her snow-white horse.

Bobby Kean could see his sweetheart with her lovely eyes of blue,
"My gal has come to meet us," he told all that cowboy crew;
But as she reached for Bobby Kean, her stallion slipped astray,
The current overturned the horse and swept them both away.

Two days men camped upon the shore and searched for Dallas
    Blue,
But neither horse nor rider ever came into their view;
Dallas' father was heartbroken, but he finally gave the word,
"There's no more use of searching and we've got to move this
    herd."

And so they came to Abilene and sold the cattle there,
Bobby Kean picked up his money and he felt the deal was fair;
Back to the famed Red River for the task he had to do,
He spent a month still searching for the gal called Dallas Blue.

His life had just one mission, no matter wrong or right,
For still a pair of pale blue eyes would haunt him every night;
He gently asked the Lord above to keep her safe and true,
The only gal he ever loved, the one called Dallas Blue.

Year after year young Bobby Kean felt sadly out of place,
From Fort Worth to El Paso, he met many a pretty face;
For those women down in Houston, words of praise are justly due,
But Bobby's heart could only love that gal called Dallas Blue.

He spent some time at ranches, but he soon would wander on,
He'd search awhile, then give up hope, and soon he would be
        gone;
For his soul was ever haunted by the bluest eyes on earth,
And he had to tell her once again just what her love was worth.

So disappointed Bobby Kean at last came home once more,
And Dallas Blue's own father met him at the ranch house door;
The men shook hands and Bobby said, "Hear what I've got to say,
To see those lovely eyes again, I've found the only way:

"My heart still reassures me there's a place where good souls go,
With God up in His heaven, Dallas waits for me, I know;
If the angels bring her back to me, then heaven is complete,
As she rides across eternity, some day our eyes will meet.

"We'll pause at the horizon, as our stallions cross the sky,
I've never loved another girl—and she's the reason why;
We'll gently kiss each other and pledge our love's still true,
A simple lonely cowboy—and a gal called Dallas Blue."

15. A Game of Roulette

Long ago near Kansas City lived a man named Dan McGowan,
He had a wife and daughter and a ranch outside of town;
But luck had turned against him in the cowboy life he chose,
He owed one thousand dollars and the bank aimed to foreclose.

So he called his wife, Marilla, and his brown-eyed daughter, Sue,
And told them both, "Our luck's turned bad, here's what I have to
    do:
I've got one hundred dollars, maybe I can win a bet,
So I'm heading into town to take my chances at roulette."

His daughter Sue responded, "Papa, you can count on me,
If there is something I can do, you know where I will be."
The smiling father then replied, "I'll keep that fact in mind
In case things go against me and I end up in a bind."

Next Dan McGowan rode into town to Bryant's Gambling Hall,
He thought, "Unless I win tonight, it's over for us all."
The owner Swifty Bryant said "McGowan, please come right in,
I hear you're short of money and roulette's where you might win."

Four times McGowan would bet his chips on number thirty-three,
Four times he lost and now he was as broke as he could be;
But Swifty Bryant looked at him, a twinkle in his eye,
"Now, Dan, I've got a special deal that still may get you by.

"You need one thousand dollars and your time is running short,
To help you in your trouble, I propose this sporting thought:
I'll bet one thousand dollars when I spin this ball of lead,
That the roulette ball will stop upon a number that is red.

"So if the number comes up red, why then of course you lose,
Then I will make but one request that you must not refuse;
For I want your daughter Susan to agree to be my wife,
It's time for me to settle down and try some married life."

"Dan stared back into Swifty's eyes and answered, 'I agree.'"

So Dan McGowan now pondered on the wisdom of this deal,
To stake his daughter's future on a spinning roulette wheel;
The last thing Sue had said was, "Papa, you can count on me."
Dan stared back into Swifty's eyes and answered, "I agree."

And now a crowd had gathered as the wheel began to spin,
"I'll earn one thousand dollars if I'm lucky and can win."
But when the ball now came to rest, it landed on the red,
And Dan McGowan reflected, "Well, I've lost and now I'm dead."

* * *

Bobby Macon was a cowboy, owned a ranch not far from town,
He often thought of Sue McGowan and of those eyes of brown;
For her to marry Swifty was a fate beyond belief,
So Bobby struck upon a plan to save her from this grief:

"Now, Swifty, you're a gambler and you like to take a chance,
So consider this proposal that I'm going to advance:
Let's try my luck, we'll spin that old roulette wheel once again,
I'll bet my ranch the number will come up from one to ten.

"But if I win, then Sue McGowan will once again be free
To marry as she pleases—she might even think of me."
Then Swifty said, "I like the odds you offer in this game,
Though Susan is as fine a gal as anyone can name."

So Swifty gives the wheel of chance another mighty spin,
The odds are almost three to one that once again he'll win;
Bobby's heart is pounding wildly but his hopes are still alive,
The wheel has stopped its spinning—and the number comes up
    five.

The crowd around the table now lets out a mighty roar,
But Bobby says to Swifty, "Will you play this game once more?
Again I'll bet my ranch the number comes up one to ten,
Against your thousand dollars if you'll try your luck again."

So Swifty answers Bobby, "Those are odds that still look good,
It's tough to bet against you, but I reckon that I should."
As wide-eyed Dan McGowan fixed Bobby Macon with a grin,
The crowd let out a rousing cheer, the ball began to spin.

Swifty Bryant stands in silence gazing at the roulette wheel,
And Macon knows the bouncing ball will soon his fate reveal;
He hopes the fickle ball will now announce that all is fine,
And once again his luck holds true—the ball hits number nine.

Next Dan McGowan slaps Macon's back as joy replaces fear,
"You've surely had a string of luck, now let's get out of here."
But Swifty says to Bobby, "How about just one more spin?"
Then Bobby shakes his head and says, "My luck is running thin."

So Bobby spoke to Dan as now together they rode home:
"I've got this thousand dollars that I offer as a loan;
I don't know how I had the guts to bet twice at roulette,
But I love your brown-eyed daughter and on her my heart is set."

So learn a lesson, partner, when your ranch is steeped in debt,
The surest way to make things worse is losing at roulette;
But if you find a faithful friend, you still may see things through,
And that's how Bobby rescued Dan—and married brown-eyed
    Sue.

16. No Day for a Hanging

Just outside of Forth Worth, Texas, rode a farmer, Lou LeMaire,
And as his buckboard rolled along, a loud cry filled the air;
A man lay stretched out in the dust, pain written on his face,
"Hey, partner, won't you help me—or I'll never leave this place."

The cowboy's leg was broken and his horse had gone astray,
So Lou dismounted from his rig to help without delay;
"I'm Jake O'Dunn, expressing thanks for dragging me to town,
I just can't make it on my own," he uttered with a frown.

So Lou found Jake a doctor and his leg was set to heal,
When people tried applauding Lou, he said, "It's no big deal."
But Jake O'Dunn was grateful while he lay there on his bed,
As Lou LeMaire was leaving, he shook his hand and said:

"There's not much now that I can do, your kindness to repay,
But times can change and so remember this is what I say:
Wherever you may travel and whatever you may see,
If ever all the chips are down, then you can count on me."

The months moved on and Lou LeMaire went courting for a wife,
He thought that lovely June LaDue could surely change his life;
The pair were strolling down the street, together lost in thought,
When suddenly two men rode up just looking for some sport.

Now Clyde and Jason Fletcher both had eyes for June LaDue,
They quickly threw a lasso and they hog-tied farmer Lou;
"Don't ever see this gal again," exclaimed the angry pair,
But then to the surprise of all, a shot now filled the air.

And there stood Jake O'Dunn, a firm expression on his face,
He quickly loosed the lasso, put the Fletchers in their place:
"If ever you try this again, I'm settling the score,
I'll let you sample both my fists, or maybe something more."

"They quickly threw a lasso and they hogtied farmer Lou."

The Fletchers hurried on their way and Jake now turned to Lou,
"You once did me a favor so again I say to you:
Wherever you may travel and whatever you may see,
If ever all the chips are down, then you can count on me."

A year passed by and Lou LeMaire had married June LaDue,
But then one day a rumor spread which turned out to be true;
For Jake O'Dunn was now in jail, a horse thief who got caught,
"And soon they're going to hang him," was what everybody
    thought.

So next the townsfolk did agree that Friday was the day,
That Jake O'Dunn would have to hang and for his crime thus pay;
But June looked at her husband and she softly said to Lou,
"That man did us a favor, is there something you can do?"

Lou sat excogitating, trying hard to find a clue,
To save a guilty horse thief's not an easy thing to do;
But then he saw the calendar and shouted out this cry,
"The day they plan to hang him is the fourth day of July!"

So they held a public meeting, noisy citizens were there,
And Lou LeMaire now raised his hand, then stood upon his chair:
"Next Friday is July the fourth, our day of liberty,
A time that's inappropriate for hanging from a tree.

"It's no day for a hanging when the flag is waving high,
It would dim the celebration if a man should have to die;
I think it only fitting—tell me if you don't agree—
In honor of our nation's birth, we set this fellow free."

So they had a consultation, some said "Yes" and some said "No,"
But finally the consensus was, "We ought to let him go.
We'll send him on his way with just a horse and traveling pack,
If on July the fourth he'll pledge, he never will come back."

Upon the holiday the townsfolk sought out Jake O'Dunn,
Who thought they'd brought the hanging rope and now his time
    had come;
Instead they said, "You're lucky it's the fourth day of July,
'Cause otherwise you'd pay the price and surely have to die."

And so they sent him down the trail to travel cross the West,
But as he left, now Lou LeMaire approached him and confessed:
"I never thought we'd see this through, so now be on your way,
Before they change their minds and lynch you on this holiday."

Just as he galloped off, Jake said these final words to Lou,
"I'll bet you're the one who saved me, once again I'm thanking
    you."
Lou handed Jake a note to look at later in the day,
"When you get ten miles further on, check what I have to say."

An hour later down the trail, "I'll rest awhile," Jake said,
He opened up Lou's farewell note—and this is what he read:
"Wherever you may travel and whatever you may see,
If ever all the chips are down, then you can count on me."

"So long, partner, till we meet again!"